HOUSE ANTHEMS

by the same author, from Valley Press

RECOVERY SONGS
HIDDEN MUSIC

RALPH DARTFORD
HOUSE ANTHEMS

Haul,

congrats

keep writing!

Ra *fo*

VP

Valley Press

First published in 2024 by Valley Press
Woodend, The Crescent, Scarborough, UK, YO11 2PW
valleypressuk.com

ISBN 978-1-915606-49-5
Cat. no. VP0240

Cover and text design by Jamie McGarry.

Printed and bound in Great Britain by
Imprint Digital, Upton Pyne, Exeter.

Contents

In loving memory of Joseph Dartford
1965 – 2022

Introduction: Houses

I can't remember much, perhaps I choose not to. It was a Spring morning in 2022 when I found out that my younger brother Joe had died. With our parents long gone too, the very first thought I had was that there was only four of us who remained. Three sons and a daughter: Frank, Geoff, April and myself. This was now our new house of reduced family.

Reflecting deeper on that day, filing its early moments of breaking news, I can still just about see and feel the sun quickening through the trees, cutting into my face and squinting my eyes. Then there was the indentation of a gentle hand on my shoulder with the soft instruction telling me to go home, to talk to friends and family and not be alone. There is a scant recollection of an offer of a taxi, but I refused and instead walked down the hill to Burley Park train station. I balanced dazed on the platform edge, stepping back as the train approached. I had to stand in the carriage on the first part of my journey which was into Leeds; the train tightly packed with rush hour passengers holding me up from falling.

I do remember taking the call from my sister, April. I can see her, phone to her ear, sitting and shaking alone at her kitchen table in her little Essex home. It was just after 7am. I was outside the hostel, vaping deeply with a cup of sweet black coffee. At the time of that call, I was mentally preparing for the early shift, the business of making doctors' appointments, dispensing washing tablets and medication to the prison men who had been released on license. The job I was doing was as a support worker in what is known officially as an 'Approved Premises'. These were halfway houses between incarceration and freedom for dangerous criminals, an opportunity of redemption and a return to some kind of normal life. The house I was working in was a Victorian mansion situated in leafy Headingley, a suburb of Leeds. Some men made it through to a different future, many didn't. I liked it there though, it was a role where I was trying to help people to get back on their feet. A continuation of my own recovery.

The phone call from my sister was brief in its bleakness and bound in confusion. Joe had been missing for a few weeks. This was not out of character for him, because he had always lived a nomadic existence. However, during that final week there had been a rise in panic as to his whereabouts. Phone calls and WhatsApp messages persisted to be unanswered. The last time I had heard from him was a month earlier, a lovely and warm birthday greeting. None of his wide circle of friends had seen or heard from him either. The police were called, and they found him in his new house in Blackpool lying on his bed. He had been dead for some time. He had apparently died of heart failure.

I say 'apparently' because for quite a while, his cause of death was clouded in chaos. There was a relentless rumour of a heroin overdose deriving from a visit from an old friend who ironically had recently absconded from another 'Approved Premises' in Basildon. This information was perhaps told to us by a distant family member. None of us are exactly sure though. My brother did not use hard drugs, he liked a spliff, we knew that, but not heroin or crack. He'd seen too many victims of addiction, including for a time, myself. However, in my early grief, I did believe that he had died from an overdose, that his escaped addict friend had visited Blackpool and given Joe a lethal dose of horror. This feeling that evil was done to my brother went on for some time, even months beyond his funeral. I wasn't alone, my sister and two brothers were also deeply suspicious.

This awful sense of unease was multiplied when that still absconded friend attended his funeral. On that day, this man tried to embrace us all with wild and flinging arms. He called our brother, "His brother". We pulled away from him in these moments, inwardly raging, on the cusp of malady, but outwardly standing in line with a united English solemnity. We had other roles to play that day: Of mourners, of hosts. Of blood family. Later, we spoke together of the fury we felt to this person who possibly could have been with Joe in his final moments, but who we found out as the months went by was not involved in his death at all. I should apologise to this man, this friend, who has now been recalled to prison for breaking the rules of not returning to the hostel that was giving him a chance of a new life. I don't know if I ever will. There is still something gnawing in me. Grief is a hallucinogenic drug all on its own.

My brother Joe was the finest of Englishmen. He was proud of the good things in our history and what we were capable of at our best. Our tolerance, kindness, open heartedness. and eccentricity. Joe had no truck with the ever-present jingoistic racism or the demonisation of people. He was a wonderful eccentric himself with a thirst for knowledge for the insanely obscure. For example, he could recite the complete 1972 bus timetable for the entire district of Basildon and the surrounding areas. He could perform this verbatim, whether you were interested or not. Joe was fanatical about buses; it was a boyhood hobby that stayed with him all his life. He collected ticket machines, posters, wing mirrors, all sorts of random items. Once, he even opened a 'Bus Museum' in my elder brother, Frank's bedroom and charged us and his school friends a 2p entrance fee for the experience. I think he was twelve years old at the time. At Joe's funeral, I read the poem 'The Bus Driver's Prayer' by his beloved Ian Dury. I know he would have demanded that.

He knew other niche things too. The history of Bluebeat and Ska music, the correct length of a turnup on a pair Levi's jeans that would determine if you were a skinhead or suedehead. Joe always said that he knew where the buried treasure was but would never tell a soul. He was completely unacademic and rarely attended school. On the rare times that he did, he was often expelled immediately for causing a riot or other outrageous misdemeanours. However, he was adored by his teachers. When news of Joe's death broke widely, an old schoolteacher wrote telling me that he was the most astonishingly bright pupil, that once when he was going through one of his 'expelled' periods, he broke into school to attend an English class because he was enjoying the book that they were reading each week. Both the English teacher and I like to think that the book is 'A Kestrel for a Knave' by Barry Hines. I hope it was because Joe idolised the character 'Billy Casper' from the book and film. He even behaved like him a lot of the time. Joe was so loved. The classic anti-hero.

The second part of my train journey on the day that Joe died was to my home in Bradford. I recall absolutely nothing about that short train trip from Leeds. I didn't go home to my flat in the centre of the city, I was numbed, disorientated and probably a danger to myself. I sent text messages, made a call to my dearest friend who was kind with guidance. I walked about for a bit, crossed roads, sat on benches and doubled back several times. I felt cold and I felt hot. I ended up in McDonald's with an untouched coffee and bun. My phone eventually rang, and it was my then ex-partner, Helen. We spoke for a minute or so and I was firmly instructed to call a taxi to go to her house, immediately, which I did. Helen's front door was open. I was safe.

When I set out to assemble this collection of poems, I wanted it to be about the house of modern England that stretches from the second half of the twentieth century to the present day. I call it a house because that is how it looks to me, a nation walled and lost in its own privacy. Of course, writing about England is not a new idea; in fact, it's almost expected of writers who live here. It's a constant obsession that will never change. Some of the poems were written before Joe's death, but most were written afterwards. The collection was not specifically meant to be about him at all, but reading the poems now, it's all about him. His astonishing spirit and enthusiasm for the country, despite everything, he loved. Furthermore, I did not realise whilst I was writing these poems that I was mourning, connecting and healing through the music and anthems of Joe's life and time. Which of course is mine too.

Ralph Dartford,
May 2024

*"Can you meet me in the country in the long grass
in the summertime in England?"*

Van Morrison

The Mourning Prayer

On days of rain, I set sail
their names. The ones I love.
It's a torrent in my palm.

Here, the rapids can engulf
my absolute blue canoe.
Here, my surfacing is at risk.

This murdered worst,
where the undertow brews
before a breaking dawn

are the moments when that love
must conjure and plead,
'You really have no choice.'

The Lark Ascending – Ralph Vaughan Williams

18th Pale Descendent

With this rusty nail
she'll carve us a tattoo.

A coloured rose
for Albion's crimes.

She'll bloom it right here
on our shoulder blades.

Let it weep
from time to time.

The Queen is Dead – The Smiths

Shame

I've tried to outstep the shame of this. Even now the guilt piles
high like records racked on an old Dansette. I was a youth lost
in a bedroom mirror, my James Brown moves flickering light
bulbs, fuelling hate in the building site politics of my father.
For this, I became his family secret, the boy who surrendered
to the funk and the darkness of 'Blues and Soul' magazine –
the cut outs of *Evelyn 'Champagne' King* sellotaped to a wall.

At after school discos I'd be staring at Floyd. His body
poured burnt treacle in a woollen hat, the greatest dancer
I have ever seen. He would beckon me over to join him,
to share our gyrations. I was good but never authentic.
How could I be? Lectured in the rudiments of old Enoch,
I walked away into the Basildon contradictions of 1977.
Punk Rock or the National Front? A question of belonging.

Confusion carried me to libraries, from Colin MacInnes
to MLK. Reciting 'The Revolution will not be Televised',
I operated inside the black and white. I routinely invaded
the southern suburbs protesting reasons for those wounded
by a lack of love, justice and connection. Some mornings,
returning home, meeting their eyes, I faced down the family
I loved through blood, but never tolerating their traditions.

And tonight, I am older in a once industrial northern town,
swooning to the music that took me, that partially unlocked
a life. I stand still from my window gazing soft at these streets
wanting to dance with every Floyd – to share our spins, our
    moments
lost in mirror balls, backflips and tepid lemonade. I can't do it!
The heavy feet of our histories still sink me beneath the floor.
How do I shed a shame of nurture? Am I late?

Shame – Evelyn 'Champagne' King

Jumping Trains

They call this room, 'The Pod'.
Outside. It's slatted, curved. A brown tortoise shell.
Inside. I distribute Mirtazapine, Tramadol, Methadone
to the rapists, murderers and others.
Sometimes it is silent. Sometimes we will talk.
Yesterday morning I was with 'Y'.
He takes a cocktail for his brain, his bones and back.
There is no family, no money, no hope of staying.
'Y' thinks he is set for Rwanda, or a return to a prison cell.
No one seems to care. Often, he sits alone weeping in the garden.
I ask him about his journey. From Eritrea to West Yorkshire.
"I jumped a train at Calais. Under the tunnel in the cold.
At home jumping trains was easy. Town to town, track to track.
It was as simple as tying a shoelace. As natural as taking a step."
'Y' says other parts were not so easy.
"Eighteen days walking through the desert.
Sixty men. Women, children and dogs.
Eighteen days and eighteen dead.
Starved, dehydrated, slashed or shot.
Days and nights without an end."
Someone in the lounge is coughing.
Someone's knocking on the door.
"Yes, jumping trains was easy."

I note his right foot has only three toes.

Jim Crow Train – Josh White

Any Old Jerusalem

On the laps of our beloved smoking mothers –
we heard them talk about the world. Of how
they were wounded when they were young.

The festooned nights of war-torn bingo halls –
where everything was just about right and unjust
about wrong. Where no one owned a phone.

How Steph danced with a Stepney Elvis.
Love me tender, love me true. The mortgage
and the factory belt. The disappointment of the pill.

Gloria and her boy from Des Moines.
That morning of God, the evening of gin.
Waving him off at Tilbury Docks. A baby in the bin.

And Julie wondering how to make ends meet.
As she pushes the roundabout, rocks the swing.
Beans and bread in a plastic bag, snagging on Terry's ring.

Yes. We can still see them on abandoned mornings –
alone with scratched blankets for their winter ghosts.
Cigarettes in mouth. Eyes down. Enraged of England.

Love Me Tender – Barb Jungr

Christmas Eve in Basildon

I remember standing
by the cold oblong bedroom
window – writing your name
in the condensation with my
index finger – praying
for the mercy of snow
that we knew would never fall.

The square below pierced
with screeched cats launching
campaigns on how to claw through
tomorrow's pregnant rubbish bins.

The Coventry Carol – Alison Moyet

Linda Blair

Waiting for the bus
after *The Exorcist*.
Your flour-caked cheeks,
my Old Spiced nicks.

Then we licked our salty lips,
from saveloy and vinegar chips.
For this we ignored the 576.
A price to pay for spring's first kiss.

Oxford Blue

I had a great big thing
with a little small-town flirt
but now she's gone away
still wearing my Oxford Blue shirt.

I bet it's not tucked in.
It's flapping around her thighs.
Top buttons coquettishly left undone
a tease for the new boy's eyes.

I'm not saying that I'm jealous.
I'm not saying that I'm hurt.
I never really cared for her.
But I loved that Oxford Blue shirt.

Favourite Shirts (Boy Meets Girl) – Haircut 100

Friday Night at Zhivago's

Stolen from him at the college disco
under a neon moon and *Tainted Love.*
The dance floor became a crime scene.
For here was the kiss of the century.

He was working at the speedway
with his petrol, his meat pies.
Planning a ruck in the North Bank.
Tomorrow was Lincoln City at home.

But she was the bee's knees of Basildon,
the peroxide princess in waiting.
Taken by the Ra Ra for a snakebite.
A half-arsed Bryan Ferry haircut.

Over the weekend she faded in Brutus jeans.
He arrived Levi jacketed, shined up boots.
The staff room tables all upturned and bloodied,
come tea break that iced Monday morning.

Rumble – Link Wray

Kid B

Radiohead
can't help you now.

As your MacBook
loses its sheen.

Breaths are sampled
through bleeped hours.

A country coughs
in twinkled green.

Nude – Radiohead

Arrowhead

Burnley late. Serrated spring
showers twist in from the west.
A Bradford train delayed as I wait –
curating my minutes of sorrow.

Earlier. Telling jokes and poems
to a room full of addicts and recoverists –
another arrowhead rain splits to a riddle.
One day at a time at this time of day?

The east bound gleamed carriages pull in.
I clutch a hankie to my face, my eyes.
An attempt to wash myself from history –
but the grit under my nail remains.

All We Want is Love – Ane Brun

The Boys with Bloodshot Eyes

He stands in front of us.
We can smell his tears.
We know this through
our own salted years
of weeping at dawn.

He arrived yesterday,
still just a boy. A boy
that wanted to be a man
for the little girl who now
has wounds inside her.

This boy, he needs sugar.
Someone to talk to about
nothing in particular.
The other residents all say,
"He's nowt more than a wrong'un."

We ask if he plays chess,
perhaps reads interesting books.
He says he draws pictures
of Jesus breaking bread,
or nailed to a blooded cross.

We enquire about his family,
who have still not been in touch.
We show him the washing machine,
how the broken shower works.
We lead him all the way. Eyes ticking time.

Open Window: Part II – Lavinia Meijer

Degrees of Difficulty

There was a girl I used to know
who would swallow dive on to her
four poster bed in times of excitement.
She'd start her run in the hallway –
ensure the matting was taped down hard.
Trips could lose her points, even smash a nose.
Afterwards, whilst smoking French cigarettes,
she'd recount other dives and falls.
The twist of hate that muscled her heart.

Jump Around – House of Pain

27

River

Grumbling Mrs. Mumble
twitching along the bridge.
Spitting spite at Canary Wharf.
Lit up like an opened fridge.

Chains jangle in the theremin wind.
Seagulls argue suicide's laugh.
Mrs. Mumble searches in pockets deep –
a dead son's photograph.

Blinking west across St Paul's –
the unbuckling of a nurse's shoe.
Mrs. Mumble stumbles into her final swim.
The forgiving and never blue.

Stephanie Mumble's boy was a sailor
who never sent a card.
His shore leave burns on a garden bonfire.
Home now and ebony charred.

River – Joni Mitchell

We Sit Under Tables

One daybreak it will be gone.
This Moon River breakfast epiphany
masquerading within its moment.

Someone will say a kind word –
or we will hear music that stitches
our reasons to beat again.

It won't be this morning.
Today's mourning is silence
and blue-choke cigarette smoke.

Joy will be taken when it comes.
As if holding these felt-tipped dolls
was just Holly Golightly in drag.

Moon River – Audrey Hepburn

House Music

3.20am. Inside this kitchen under emergency fluorescents.
Head in hands – elbows on polished, scratched aluminum.
I scan the clocks. Thinking I'm already tired for tomorrow –
the beige days that will come long at me again.

It's almost so quiet. The hums of fridges, maybe rats outside
on a feed. Hours ago, I called the lucky winning numbers
in the lounge for the weekly Friday night 'Sex Offender Bingo'.
There were prizes of coat hangers, chocolate buttons and crisps.

They sleep above now in their soft-walled rooms with thin duvets,
angry sticky wet dreams fogged by two-for-one deodorant.
They can't see me here, in tears. Freed by the prayers I whisper.
Men. We are all a flicked switch from black. A twitch from evil.

Scary Monsters (And Super Creeps) – David Bowie

A Bookseller Unlocks

Bradford street cold
pigeon grey with rain.
The huddled threaten Waterstones
with language and needles.

Inside, these unlit pages
could bake them cakes,
instruct the rules of golf,
send them all to Mandalay.

Or ignite to keep love warm.

Hey Jack Kerouac – 10,000 Maniacs

Mark Hollis

You came with morning.
Then every dawning after.
Freshened. New grass. Life.

A New Jerusalem – Mark Hollis

The January Rebellion

The dishwasher is reading Kafka.
The toaster has taken to drink.
The freezer has joined the picket line.
The whole kitchen is in the sink.

Private Revolution – World Party

A Question Concerning Stephanie Mumble

Erm... Yes... Come in.

I was just making something to eat.
Would you like a cup of tea?
We don't get many of your sort around here.
Yes. I know money is tight these days.

Well. She lived opposite
at number thirty-two.
Didn't really know her.
We minded our own business.

Anything strange? Not really.

Actually, there was one thing
She would wait at the window,
stare down our street
every second of the month
with all her windows open –
whatever the weather.
We all used to watch her.
It became a regular occurrence.

Oh. Another thing.

She'd get angry at the leaves,
the plastic bags, hooked on trees.
She would walk out shouting,
"Where are you? Where is he?"
She'd be waving her broom, spitting in the mud.
It looked like she was sweeping up the world.

My school friend, Jack,
now he was scared of her. Not me. I wasn't.
Jack's dead now.
No, I thought her name was Daphne.

Hour by the hour, she'd work.
Front garden to back,
kerb to drain,
she was obviously in pain.

When it finally snowed,
as it did in those days.
She would lock herself in,
gaze out at us in wonder,
then fury when it thawed.
The windows still open though.
Yes, that is all I knew of her.
She left here many years ago.
No, no Constable.
I didn't know she had a son.

Oh. How sad.
She must have been freezing.

Changes – Nils Frahm

Otis

Somewhere tonight in the hard
light of a northern town
solitude sits on a sofa
with the dim light of a quarter 'till three.
Tired and lost to love,
tried in the couldn't be.

He smokes cigarettes
with black coffee,
plays precious music
and dreams a dance.
A step away into tomorrow's glare,
yet further removed from chance.

Cigarettes and Coffee – Otis Redding

The Ballad of St. John's Square

Sky white as good Afghan heroin.
A prelude to snow on the wind.
The chestnut tree hisses blind panic –
her fruits never bargained for this.

> Sunday church bells ring Jazz out for Jesus.
> It's Mary's last night alone in the choir.
> She's fallen in love with the verger, you see –
> even though she knows he's a liar.

Mr Johnson stands in his doorway,
at the wonderment of news taking flight.
His dog Raffles howls for his mission –
but the cats have crept home for the night.

> The first flake falls upon the black car,
> where nervous Terry fidgets inside.
> Carnations splayed out on her back seat –
> begging for Julie to let go of her pride.

Now the conkers are falling as if maces.
Boys field whoppers with stealth in the slips.
The branches bow down to the blizzard –
shadow dancing along to her whips.

> And here's lost Arif traipsing the graveyard.
> A Chicken Korma and rice to deliver.
> *Louise Marston Rest in Peace* –
> He was there that day at the river.

The Verger and Mary are all tangled.
The empty pews reverentially hushed.
Smoking from a pack of Marlboro Lights –
naked and sweet Sherry blushed.

Arif knocks hard on Johnston's red door.
Teary eyed and neon ice blue.
"Come inside, we'll warm you up –
although Raffles prefers Vindaloo."

Bells fall silent at last for a denouement.
Terry and Julie have a plane to catch.
They've just set bleeding hallway ablaze –
history books to a red stroking match.

And thirty-seven rattles in the corner.
Thirty-eight holds a glass to the wall.
Thirty-nine steps out for a new England.
And at number forty; I'm recording it all.

Go My Heart, Go to Heaven – Shabaka and The Ancestors

Mexico 70

There were rumours
of decimalisation
at Manor House Junior school.

It was the summer of 1970,
of Esso World Cup coins –
free with a tenner of four star.

My Dad didn't own a car.

My best friend's name was Zolly.
He had a Rediffusion colour TV.
A yelping dog called Bugsy,
his soft-bosomed mum made my shy.

And Rosa taught me to dance
and swallow a pickled herring.
She wore her world in possibilities.
Just like Pele's final pass.

Eso y más – Joan Sebastian

Fodder

A town in the south. A March Saturday night. A little bistro that serves pasta dishes to Terry and Julie. She is all twin set nostalgia. He is slacks and Argyle fantasies. They talk of new austerity, muddling through, carrying on. There is always the rugby, their pals at The Ship. A pint in a tankard – just a small sherry for control. There's the up-and coming production of Oklahoma at the Civic Theatre for Julie. She's been a local operatic for years, started out in the chorus – now promoted to playing the lead. That Christmas card did the trick. Terry makes the props, pushes the scenery around, the dancers a little too much.

At the all-night garage on the edge of this town, Hardeep takes a punch in the ribs for running out of bread and Rizla. Kebab fuelled boys' piss on today's newspapers, vomit on the forecourt. Not far away, outside a lighted house, in a road in this town she should never be in. A Bacardi breezed girl with Winehouse hair lifts her skirt for a line of coke, the promise of love. Inside that house, the net curtains twitch. Terry and Julie's permanent itch, forever sore. Look further, a framed portrait – pouted and poised. This is still Margaret's. A little winced country.

Old England – The Waterboys

The Joke Isn't Funny Anymore

He loved the comic,
Bob Monkhouse.

Especially the joke about folk
laughing when Bob said he wanted

to be a comedian and not
laughing now that he was.

She tried to laugh with him for years,
but here, on her new wedding

day, she giggles at him
applauding alone in his cell.

Don't Rain on My Parade – Barbra Streisand

As the Last Train Pulls Away

lighting
thunder
wind
and
snow

under
the railway
bridge
she
will
go

to
freeze
beneath
witches
that
don't
want
to
know

of
her
lightning
thunder
wind
and
snow.

Don't Want to Know – John Martyn

Careless

If I asked you while this sun
dripped its blood
into a brown-loathed sea
what the worst words were.

You would perhaps shrug your
shoulders – look at your shoes.
It's not *I don't love you.*
It's not even *I hate you.*

I would say the worst words –
when all is red and rusted –
when the tide retreats to reveal
our shells, will be, *I don't care.*

Maybe you'd tighten those laces
                          then
                      softly
                   skip
                away.

Unless – The Pale Fountains

Other Colours, Other Clocks

A summer funeral home in a pound shop Essex town.
The flowers are chemical, the doves bleached pigeons.
We are a family in fabricated grief, gasping at heated facts,
tasting an electrical breeze. "There was bloody water down
his sink and ripped up reminders surrounding his bin."
Here is love's finality, its knife, needle and rumour mill –
scarring the skin of what we believed possible within his life.
Now we are four children. Bewildered, glued together by photo
albums and staring at each other's shoes. Our memory fused
by his sleight of hand street corner card trick con. He is gone,
and tonight alone, a deep ticking will quicken into our private
rooms, cutting time into slices to be served on other clocks.
  Come Christmas, we'll know this for sure.
  How we followed his star. Our feet red raw.

Family Life – The Blue Nile

England's Dreaming

I was telling Gareth Southgate
only this morning about
the convenience
of having my weekly
train ticket on my phone.

He said that I had made
a sensible choice.

He was also pleased
that I make myself a ham
and pickle sandwich for my lunch.
Although he suggested
the occasional Scotch Egg.

We skipped down the lane to the station.
July's cornflowers choking
June's poppies to death again.
Our hands were almost touching.

Gareth sniffed at the horizon,
told me that rain can appear knowing
on the days we fall in love.

"It can be warm, cool, or lush –
a comfort inside our madness."

We both recited some poetry.
Of Adlestrop, birds
and Gloucestershire.

I asked him about the penalties.
Gareth said he was trying to make a point.

Summertime in England – Van Morrison

Geese

Across an England October zinc
sky, they come. Sketched at angles
as if to resemble flags dragged.
The Geese are migrating.

Rain falls and I shake from news
of other migrants panicking south.
A red, green and white land blackened.
Their lives weighted to hell or heaven?

Hang Clouds – Sue Verran and Evelyn Glennie

Codes

From Dewsbury Moor to New Orleans –
Frosty Jack – Romanian Bourbon.
Filleted skunk swooned upon a breeze –
all mustard lit in white urban.

We rage hard on tongue come toothless codes.
Offer kisses then ball up our fists.
Short odds between a frog and a toad –
you're either tossed or crossed off our list.

Ghost Town (Extended Version) – The Specials

Mayday

The first bee of spring
swerves in a garden unkempt
by winter and the dead.
I stand at this back door –
shaken, considering the two sunflowers
of our now excavated summer.

I recall yet another relentless bee
that fed on heat's luxurious languor.
Oh honey! We all have a sting in our tale.

Tramp the Dirt Down – Elvis Costello

Latitude: -23.6975. Longitude: 133.8836.

Here, in this ruined red world
truth and news are under exposed
for the purpose of discoloration.

Locals sneer in English,
restrict oxygen to the indigenous,
struggle with words like *generous*.

Convenience forgets kindness,
buries bones that won't grow.
Here is nothing but theirs.

This Bitter Earth – Dinah Washington

Merge

I'm scanning documents.
Evaluation reports from the boys.

        Their handwriting is broken, literacy poor –
        but they seemed to enjoy it. Two hours

with the chance to read and write
their reduced aspirations.

        A colleague says just merge them
        into a single document. "That'll do."

But they can't be merged, can they?
They will always be unlike you and me

        despite our everything else. They have the bad
        luck of wrongdoing – of just getting caught.

Yes. These boys deserve a place here.
A place in the sun as well as the rain.

Swimmer

Land, where are you now?
This queasy, diseased sea
has anchored her deep.

She swallows in salted water.
Chokes on petrol, chooses stars –
smashes the surf with fists.

Lord! Where are you now?
Your remiss promise of shore leave.
The swim to Europe's end.

England – PJ Harvey

Act!

Looking from the window above, like a story of love. Can you hear me?
– Yazoo, 'Only You', 1982

And, you know, there's no such thing as society.
– Margaret Thatcher, 1987

I'm lonely here. There are no poets here. Oh yes, one or two. There's always one or two but, mostly only makers of money.
– Arnold Wesker, Beorhtel's Hill, *A play for Basildon*, 1989

We were the great experiment. The babies born wild into this
   new Jerusalem.
Our blameless, fucked-up parents dragged onto fast-tracked
   conveyor belts –
delivering us all screaming in bloodied ragged beauty. Our
   birthmarks exposed.
The town planners, in celebratory shock, coughed bile from
   cheap tipped cigarette
fumes, got pissed blind on tepid Watney's Party 7 whilst
   snapping Harold Wilson's
pipe and singing 'World Cup Willie'. Here was their fortune.
   Here was our future made.

This was Basildon. A strangeloved Formica futurist Essex
   delta dream paved
with pearly lined, brutalist estates and never-ending pursuits
   of Green Shield stamps.
Our East Ended mums and dads arriving on promises of
   indoor toilets and hope,
of working hard in the new factories, shopping centres and
   breeze blocked building
sites, forever gazing back at a beloved estuary. Out of time
   now and out of reach.
For now, there were new names for them to conjure:
   Craylands, Pitsea, Alcatraz.

In pushchairs we were trundled along as if prizes in a town
  centre parade. The shops,
the fountain. Sharp light, dull talk. Cold, hot, fog. A clock
  like a billiard ball ticking
as if chance was running slow and out already, compressing
  the wins, the losses.
We'd have rubber sandwiches in cafes that played chirpy
  cheap beautiful pop music.
In the aisles of Sainsbury's, Timothy Whites and the cut price
  mince merchants
of the shouting market, we'd always be looking and listening.
  The early notes.

At school, we coloured in castles, staged wars in playgrounds.
  Failed at kiss chase.
Sometimes we'd pose at the seaside. Cockles, muscles and cut
  glass on the shore.
We never saw a black boy or girl, except Cassius Clay or
  Diana Ross on the telly.
When two arrived in the classroom, we played with them as
  if they were toys.
They never came to our birthday parties, we'd never see them
  on a Saturday morning.
Confused to the reasons we made enquiries, got clipped ears
  when asking for more.

Elsewhere, on the other side, beyond the refinery, in the
  garden parties
of a confident older England, Mick Jagger sang of untidy
  Kentish wives with
19 nervous breakdowns and clutched blister packs of
  mother's little helpers.
And in Liverpool, another estuary. The Beatles swooned
  triumphant of love
and a diamond encrusted Lucy's murmuration into a Mersey
  dockland sky.
Here, in this Basildon, we could not even hold a tune. Not
  yet. Not for a while.

The trains stopped at our town in 1974. Our new station was
like Cape Canaveral.
Tickets to London, a journey to Mars or Jupiter, Petticoat
Lane and Upton Park.
In 1976 the roads melted. We wrote our names in the tarmac,
squinted in sweat
as we learned wood and metal, how to bake a cake, stitch
and sew into our tomorrows.
In Raquel's discotheque dancing to Travolta, kissing under
the palm tree a girl got pregnant.
Then the holidays to Benidorm. The bullfighting posters on
our walls. A ballet of death.

We were happy in parts. Our town immune and tranquilized.
A glass, concrete peace.
On the telly again, young men with bad teeth told a goading
presenter to "Fuck Off!".
Questions in the House of Commons about bringing back the
birch and National Service.
In our houses we went to our bedrooms. John Peel and
anarchy giving us enough rope
to became NF, Soulboys or Punks. Creation quickening inside
us. Finally, the song to sing.
Then came "Where there is discord may we bring harmony."
The chrysalis cracked.

Outside of here, there was a war, unemployment, strikes and
riots. But they loved her.
In Basildon, her trick was to divide and rule. Buy your home,
be better than your neighbour.
Our parents became competitive and mean. A hurricane blew
hate and our houses down.
We acted in plays, formed bands in our kitchens, brought
keyboards from toy shops.
We signed on the dole, wore long coats, ate beans on toast in
front of Top of the Pops
as one of our own gazed from the screen. If they can do this,
then why can't we?

The town began to fold in. A plastic Barclaycarded Royal
  Flush busted to debt in the shops,
satellite TV and laminated flooring. Us, the artists were
  viewed with suspicion, a luxury carpet
only we rolled on. No one invited us to our theatre, our
  library. A place in the world.
Other popstars came here. The kids waiting twice around the
  block, singing their hits.
We got drunk on disappointment in the pubs. Ecstasy came
  and a young girl died of thirst.
Our own Top of the Pops band became the biggest in the
  world. They never spoke of us.

Some of us left for London, some headed north, south and
  west. Some put down their pens
and synthesisers. They gave up their good. Disappointment is
  the greatest heartbreak of all.
A few fought. A resistance against the power of disinterest. A
  puppeteer here, a poet there.
These were the troubadours that time forgot, but time does
  not care about their feelings.
Basildon. The future has faded like a record, the needle
  popping and jumping as if a message.
The tribute bands rule, the shops boarded up, heads are
  down. But our story must continue.

Artists of Basildon! It's innate to create. No one is going to
  gift you, so gift yourself.
Take your purpose proud, fight for it with absolute love. Act
  now, not tomorrow!
We, the ones who came before demand this. We lived in this
  town and perhaps do still.
So, paint, sing, write, dance, bang that drum in the estates,
  the streets, the pubs and shops.
Take clay, mould it with truth, bake it hard until
  unbreakable. Cement a future new.
Deliver that screaming bloodied ragged beauty. Hand it on.
  Reach out and touch faith!

Across Clapham Common

And I walk alone
in a city wept of its men
and what we do.

Last week, in early Spring,
I'd cock my head, maybe smile.
But here, a Crocus. I'll retreat.

Walk Away Renee – The Four Tops

Brass

For us, there were journeys of fine weather between
the walled towns. But now, it rains inside our trains.
Once, our days and nights tapped out hot rhythms
as we danced mambas drenched in salted sweat –
dipped our dreams with blistered fingers –
raised life's hopes to the turncoat wind.
In teatime kitchens, our chips drowned in gravy
and nothing of comfort's good came calling.
These streets have been forsaken by forensics –
the small price of power's broken bicycle.
Hills are now histories. No miners. No steel
as we live a slag-heap northern slander.
Twice and thrice, that 'us' has become
hopeless, hapless and ice cold homespun.
Yes. We live in the walled towns
where the red flag frays flaccid.
  Where our brass bands
  have stopped carousing.

Love Will Tear Us Apart – The Hot 8 Brass Band

Ways

And I'm remembering my friend Stevie
on that early train to London town.
Learning the words to 'True Love Ways'
for his open audition for *Buddy. The Musical.*
Nan's heavy magnified glasses in his top pocket,
an overnight bag just in case they want
him for tomorrow's matinee. He'll be ready.

And I sigh for Julie in Somerset, long gone.
Her key under the mat every night, thinking that he just
might call. A bottle of Metaxa brandy under his arm, the tall
tales of indiscretions in high office, knowing his fists
are unclenched and withering now – will be forever more.
Their headstones rest unevenly up there on the levels.
Opposites always attract their true love ways.

And I'm drifting towards my mother and father
holding on to Christmas for dear life. Money borrowed
for bicycles, radios, Quality Street tins. The first week
of January, the never-never knocking through the door.
The once filled ashtrays turned, loose change found down
the sofa. The plates smashed; a bad cheque cashed until February
pays for the morning sickness. The consequences of ways.

And finally, I wake myself writing these words in Bradford.
Sitting here, listening to myself for the first time in months.
A glass of time, a scented candle. A prayer in their names –
etched into the palm of my shaking hand thrice again.
A flame always flickers its death, the hot wax rubs my memory.
Stevie sings into eternity as the audience falls from the gods.
Love weighs true if you balance faith long enough.

True Love Ways – Buddy Holly

The Evening Prayer

Brother. There is still time for us
to wipe our tongues across greying lips
and kiss the world back.

For you were no different than me.
I have committed the crimes too.
Show us both a denier, we'll give you a liar.

We have judged each other on the streets,
on our phones, in their churches.
The sacred was for pillaging.

But sleep now, brother. Dream wild
with me and I will write your name again.
Joseph. It's not too late to steal time.

Bus Drivers' Prayer – Ian Dury

Acknowledgements

'Across Clapham Common' was first published in the anthology *Masculinity*, Broken Sleep Books, 2024.

'Shame' was a commission for Bradford Literature Festival 2022, and subsequently published in Magma 89 in 2024.

'The January Rebellion' and 'Latitude: -23.6975. Longitude: 133.8836.' were first published in the anthology *The Apocalyptic Landscape,* Valley Press, 2024

'Act!' was a commission for Basildon's 'The Great Gathering' project, 2024. The film of the poem, with music composed by Gary Clark, can be seen (and heard) by searching 'ACT! A POEM FOR BASILDON' on YouTube.com.

'Degrees of Difficulty' was first published in Annie Journal, 2023.

'Brass' was first published in Prole 35, 2024.

'Oxford Blue' was first published in the pamphlet *Cigarettes, Beer and Love*, Ossett Observer Presents, 2017.

With an enormous thank you to the following:
The Royal Literature Fund, Cardigan House Approved Premises in Leeds and my wonderful colleagues at The National Literacy Trust.

Steve Ely, Michael Stewart and Gavin Jones at the University of Huddersfield. Jonny Syer and Nick Jones at northerngravy. com. Dan Thompson, Gary Clark, Clare Shaw, Sarah Wimbush, Mike Farren, Mick Jenkinson, Katy Mahon, Ian Parks, Peter Pegnall, David Willis, Russ Litten, David Floyd, Roger Robinson, Amanda Huggins, Steve Whitaker, Louise Fazackerley, Kate Fox, Helen Ivory, Martin Figura, Brett Evans, Jamie Thrasivoulou, Vicky Foster, Emma King, Jill and Phil Adam, Gary and Jean Horsman.

Liz, Will, Sienna and Faith Martel for days and nights of laughter and love.

My family, who held true in a time of despair.

My great friend, Jacqui Wicks. Years go by.

The Reverends Emma Wilkinson and Laity Watters. Have faith in the young!

Helen, my wife, who opened her door.

'House Anthems: A Playlist by Ralph Dartford' is available to listen to on Apple Music and Spotify.

The house I was born in.